1

This is a work of fiction. Names, characters, places and incidents either are products of the author's imagination or are used fictitiously.

Table of Contents

The Prisoner

As the clock ticked down to the New Year, the Fletcher household buzzed with anticipation. Suitcases were packed, plans were made, and the promise of a fresh start hung in the air. But for one member of the family, the arrival of 2022 brought no such hope. Lacey Fletcher, a prisoner in her own home, could only listen as her family prepared to leave her behind, trapped in a nightmarish existence that defied comprehension.

Confined to a couch that had become her whole world, Lacy's once vibrant life had been reduced to a hellish cycle of neglect and despair. The young woman who had once dreamed of a bright future now faced a bleak reality, her body ravaged by the unimaginable horrors inflicted upon her. As her family eagerly anticipated the festivities of New Year's Eve, Lacey was left to wonder if she would even survive the night.

The depths of Lacy's suffering were almost too much to bear. Hungry and alone, she sat naked and covered in her own filth, unable to move or care for herself. The couch that had once provided comfort had become a prison, her flesh melting into the leather as she slowly wasted away. The stench of decay hung heavy in the air, a sickening reminder of the slow death that consumed her.

But even as her body deteriorated, Lacy's mind remained trapped in a never-ending cycle of fear and desperation. Would her family remember to leave her food and water? Would they even come back at all? The thought of being left to starve or succumb to dehydration was almost too much to contemplate. And even if they did return, what kind of life awaited her? A existence defined by pain, humiliation, and the unrelenting march of time.

As the hours ticked by and the New Year's Eve festivities reached their climax, Lacey may have heard the distant sound of fireworks, a cruel reminder of the world beyond her prison. But for her, there was no celebration, no hope of a better tomorrow. Instead, she was left to endure the agony of her own deteriorating body, her flesh rotting away as maggots feasted on the decaying tissue.

The extent of Lacy's injuries was almost too horrific to comprehend. Gaping holes peppered her lower body, exposing the stark white of her bones beneath. Her once healthy skin had become a mottled patchwork of sores and scars, a testament to the years of neglect and abuse she had endured. And perhaps most disturbingly of all, her stomach contained not food, but the foam of the couch cushions and the feces that had become her constant companions.

As investigators would later discover, Lacy's ordeal had spanned an astonishing 12 years. More than a decade of her life had been stolen away, her hopes and dreams shattered by the unimaginable cruelty of those who were supposed to love and protect her. And even as the authorities began to unravel the mystery of her case, one question loomed larger than all the rest: why? What could possibly drive a family to subject their own flesh and blood to such unimaginable torment?

But as the New Year dawned and the world moved on, Lacey remained trapped in her own personal hell, a prisoner of the couch and a victim of the most heinous kind of abuse. Her story serves as a chilling reminder of the depths of human cruelty and the unimaginable suffering that can be inflicted upon the most vulnerable among us. And as we grapple with the horror of her ordeal, we are left to wonder how such a thing could have happened, and what justice, if any, can ever be served.

As the harrowing tale of Lacey Fletcher's prolonged ordeal unfolds, one question looms large in the minds of those who seek to understand the unfathomable: what could have possibly driven her family to subject her to such unimaginable torment? The answers, it seems, remain shrouded in mystery, leaving us to grapple with a range of theories that attempt to shed light on this darkest of crimes.

One possibility that has emerged is the notion of locked-in syndrome, a rare neurological condition in which a person remains fully conscious but unable to move or communicate due to complete paralysis of nearly all voluntary muscles. In this scenario, Lacey may have been a prisoner not only of her own home but of her own body, trapped inside her mind as the world around her descended into a living nightmare. The thought of enduring such a fate for even a day is enough to send shivers down one's spine, but to imagine the agony of being locked in for over a decade is truly beyond comprehension.

Yet another theory that has taken hold in the minds of those who seek to unravel this enigma is the possibility of full-blown torture, with Lacey serving as the unwitting victim of a twisted individual's sadistic pleasures. The idea that someone could take perverse joy in subjecting another human being to such unimaginable suffering is a chilling reminder of the depths of depravity that lurk within the human psyche. And while we may recoil at the thought of such cruelty, the fact remains that cases of prolonged torture and abuse are all too common in the annals of true crime.

Of course, these are just two of the myriad theories that have emerged in the wake of Lacy's tragic demise. Some have suggested that her family may have been suffering from a severe case of mental illness, unable to comprehend the gravity of their actions or the toll they were taking on their helpless victim. Others have pointed to the possibility of financial motivations, with Lacy's disability checks serving as a twisted incentive for her continued confinement and neglect.

But regardless of the underlying motives, one thing remains abundantly clear: Lacey Fletcher suffered one of the most slow, torturous deaths imaginable, and nobody stepped forward to help her. The fact that she could endure such unimaginable agony for so long, with no one intervening to put an end to her misery, is a damning indictment of a society that all too often turns a blind eye to the suffering of its most vulnerable members.

Locked-In Syndrome

One theory that has emerged is the possibility that she may have been suffering from a rare and terrifying condition known as locked-in syndrome.

For those afflicted with locked-in syndrome, the experience is akin to being trapped within one's own body, a prisoner of the mind with no way to escape. The mind continues to race at a frenetic pace, thoughts and emotions swirling in an endless loop, but the body remains unresponsive, unable to translate those impulses into action. In some cases, sufferers may retain the ability to open their eyes and move their pupils, offering a glimpse into the world around them, but even this small mercy is often denied.

The terror of locked-in syndrome lies not only in the physical paralysis but in the inability to communicate with the outside world. Imagine the frustration and desperation of trying to speak, to cry out for help, only to have the words die in your throat, trapped behind uncooperative lips and tongue. It's a nightmare scenario that has haunted the imaginations of people for generations, a fear that strikes at the very core of what it means to be human.

For those lucky enough to survive the initial onset of locked-in syndrome, the prognosis is grim. The vast majory of sufferers die within the first 3 months, their bodies unable to cope with the stress and strain of the condition. Even for those who do survive, the road to recovery is long and arduous, with no guarantee of ever regaining the ability to move or communicate.

In Lacey Fletcher's case, the possibility of locked-in syndrome adds an even more tragic dimension to an already horrific tale of abuse and neglect. If she was indeed suffering from this condition, trapped within her own body as the world around her descended into a living hell, the agony of her final years is almost too much to contemplate. The thought of being unable to cry out for help, to beg for mercy, as one's own family members subject them to unimaginable torment is a fate worse than death itself.

Of course, the presence of locked-in syndrome in Lacy's case remains purely speculative at this point, and it is possible that other factors may have played a role in her prolonged confinement and suffering. But even if this theory proves unfounded, the mere possibility of such a condition serves as a chilling reminder of the fragility of the human body and the depths of suffering that can be inflicted upon it.

It is imperative that all possible angles be explored, including the potential role of locked-in syndrome in her tragic fate.

We will, hopefully, get to the bottom of this in the course of this book.

Voices from Within

As the specter of locked-in syndrome looms over the tragic case of Lacey Fletcher, the accounts of those who have survived this terrifying condition offer a chilling glimpse into the unimaginable suffering that may have defined her final years. These voices from within, trapped inside unresponsive bodies, paint a picture of a living nightmare, a hell on earth that defies comprehension.

A male survivor described the torment of locked-in syndrome compounded by the physical agony that accompanied it. Trapped in a body that was excruciatingly sensitive to even the slightest sensory changes, he could describe the sensation of his skin burning, as though it were on fire, and the constant, unrelenting pain that consumed him. "I was completely at the mercy of my doctors for pain meds," he might recall, the helplessness and desperation still raw in his voice.

But perhaps even more agonizing than the physical torment was the psychological toll of being trapped within one's own body, unable to communicate even the most basic of needs. "I couldn't tell anyone if my mouth was dry, if I was hungry, if I had an itch that needed to be scratched," the survivor might confess, the anguish of those long, lonely hours still etched into his memory. "I felt disgusting all the time."

To cope with the unimaginable isolation and despair, some survivors of locked-in syndrome have reported creating internal dialogues, entire conversations carried out within the confines of their own minds. One man spoke of inventing a second voice, a companion to help him navigate the long, empty hours and stave off the ever-present fear of being trapped inside his body forever.

For Lacey Fletcher, the possibility that she may have endured a similar fate, trapped within a body that had become a prison, adds an even more tragic dimension to an already horrific tale. If she was indeed suffering from locked-in syndrome, unable to communicate her pain and terror as her family members subjected her to unimaginable neglect and abuse, the true extent of her suffering may never be fully known.

It is imperative that we consider all possible explanations for her prolonged ordeal, including the potential role of locked-in syndrome. By doing so, we may be able to shed light on the untold stories of countless others who have suffered in silence, trapped within the confines of their own bodies and minds.

And while the accounts of those who have survived locked-in syndrome offer a glimmer of hope, a testament to the resilience and strength of the human spirit, they also serve as a stark reminder of the unimaginable suffering that can be inflicted upon the most vulnerable among us. As we seek to unravel the mysteries surrounding Lacey Fletcher's tragic fate, let us never forget the voices from within, the silent screams of those who have endured the unendurable, and the urgent need to ensure that no one else is ever left to suffer in silence again.

The road to diagnosis and treatment is often a long and agonizing one, fraught with uncertainty and despair.

In many cases, the first glimmer of hope comes in the form of a simple blink, a subtle movement of the eyes that hints at the presence of a fully conscious mind trapped inside a paralyzed body. For the doctors and nurses tasked with caring for these patients, the realization that they may be dealing with a case of locked-in syndrome is a moment of both terror and relief, a chance to finally establish a line of communication with a patient who has been suffering in silence for far too long.

But even after a diagnosis is made, the road ahead is far from easy. As a survivor discovered, the process of learning to communicate through eye movements or other subtle signals can be a slow and frustrating one, requiring patience, persistence, and an unwavering determination to be heard.

The survivor found solace in the constant presence of his family, who never left his side throughout his ordeal. But even their love and support could not ease the profound sense of loneliness that consumed him, the knowledge that no one could truly understand the depth of his suffering or the frustration of being unable to communicate his most basic needs and desires.

As the scientific community continues to search for new ways to diagnose and treat locked-in syndrome, stories like these serve as a powerful reminder of the urgent need for better tools and technologies to help these patients communicate with the world around them. From cutting-edge brain-computer interfaces to simple devices that allow patients to spell out words and phrases through eye movements alone, the field of locked-in syndrome research is one of constant innovation and progress.

But even as we celebrate these advances, we must never forget the human toll of this devastating condition, the countless lives that have been lost or irrevocably altered by its cruel and unyielding grip. For every survivor, there are countless others who have suffered in silence, their stories untold and their voices forever lost to the void.

As we reflect on the tragic case of Lacey Fletcher and the many unanswered questions that surround her final years, let us also remember the brave and resilient individuals who have fought their way back from the brink of locked-in syndrome, who have found a way to make their voices heard in a world that had all but forgotten them. Theirs is a story of hope and perseverance, a testament to the unbreakable spirit of the human mind and the power of love and compassion to light the way through even the darkest of times.

The Enigma

As the shocking revelations surrounding the tragic case of Lacey Fletcher began to unravel in 2022, the true crime community found itself grappling with a mystery that defied conventional explanation. Rumors had been circulating since 2020 about a young woman from Louisiana who had seemingly been trapped in a living nightmare, confined to her couch for an astonishing 12 years before finally succumbing to her inexplicable fate.

But as more details emerged about Lacy's case, it became increasingly clear that the true nature of her ordeal was far more complex and disturbing than anyone had initially imagined. For unlike the victims of locked-in syndrome, whose paralysis could be attributed to a cruel twist of neurological fate, Lacey appeared to be an able-bodied woman in the prime of her life, with no apparent physical or medical reason for her prolonged immobility.

The idea that a healthy, competent individual could remain fixed in place for more than a decade, eschewing all human contact and interaction, was one that challenged the very foundations of our understanding of human behavior and psychology. What could possibly account for such a profound and perplexing state of catatonia, and what did it say about the hidden depths of the human psyche?

A range of disturbing theories and possibilities began to emerge. Some speculated that she may have been the victim of a rare and undiagnosed mental illness, one that had slowly eroded her will and capacity to engage with the world around her. Others suggested that she may have been subjected to a form of psychological manipulation and abuse that had left her powerless to resist or escape, trapped in a web of coercive control that had gradually consumed her entire existence.

But perhaps the most chilling aspect of Lacy's case was the fact that, by all appearances, she had not been physically restrained or confined in any way. There were no chains, no locks, no barriers that had kept her tethered to that fateful couch for all those years. Instead, it seemed that something far more sinister and intangible had been at work, a force that had slowly drained away her autonomy and agency, leaving her a hollow shell of her former self.

It became clear that the true scope of Lacy's suffering may never be fully known or understood. The years of isolation and neglect had taken a devastating toll on her body and mind, leaving behind a broken and emaciated figure that bore little resemblance to the vibrant young woman she had once been.

But even in the face of such unimaginable tragedy, the search for answers and accountability continues. For Lacey Fletcher, and for all those whose lives have been cut short by the dark and twisted forces that lurk within the human heart, the quest for justice and understanding must never waver or falter.

The Aldermen of Slaughter

Nestled in the heart of Louisiana, the diminutive town of Slaughter is a place where the bonds of community run deep and the spirit of neighborly compassion is woven into the very fabric of daily life. With a population of just 800 souls, this close-knit hamlet is the kind of place where everyone knows everyone else's name, and where the trials and tribulations of one are shared by all.

But despite its idyllic veneer, Slaughter is no stranger to the darker currents of human experience. Its very name, though derived from the original landowners rather than any grim historical event, seems to hint at the unspoken shadows that can lurk beneath even the most placid of surfaces.

At the center of this intricate tapestry of relationships and shared history stand the

Aldermen, a group of elected officials who serve as the beating heart of Slaughter's civic life. These benign figures are more than just bureaucrats or politicians; they are the confidants, the advisors, and the shoulders to cry on for an entire community.

Whether it's a lost pet that needs tracking down, a disabled resident in need of better accessibility, or even a deeply personal crisis that threatens to tear a family apart, the people of Slaughter know that they can always turn to their Aldermen for guidance and support. These are the individuals who have been entrusted with the sacred duty of safeguarding the well-being of their neighbors, and who work tirelessly to ensure that no one in their charge is left to face life's challenges alone.

But even the most vigilant of guardians can be caught off guard by the depths of human suffering and despair. And so it was that the Aldermen of Slaughter found themselves confronted with a tragedy that would test the very limits of their compassion and resolve.

The case of Lacey Fletcher, a young woman who had seemingly vanished from the world for over a decade, only to be discovered in a state of unimaginable neglect and degradation, sent shockwaves through the tight-knit community of Slaughter. How could such a thing have happened under their watchful eyes? How could a vulnerable member of their flock have slipped through the cracks, left to waste away in agony and isolation?

As the details of Lacey's ordeal began to emerge, the people of Slaughter were forced to grapple with some uncomfortable truths about the limits of their own awareness and the ways in which even the most well-intentioned of communities can fail to see the suffering that lurks in their midst.

For the Aldermen, the weight of this tragedy was particularly heavy. As the elected representatives of the people, they couldn't help but feel a sense of responsibility for what had happened to Lacey. Had they missed the signs of her distress? Had they failed to provide the kind of support and intervention that might have saved her from such a horrific fate?

These were the questions that would haunt the Aldermen in the weeks and months to come, as they struggled to come to terms with the enormity of what had transpired under their watch. And yet, even in the face of such darkness, they knew that they could not succumb to despair or cynicism.

For the people of Slaughter, the Aldermen represented a beacon of hope and resilience in an often uncertain world. And so, as the community began the long and painful process of healing and reconciliation, the

Aldermen redoubled their efforts to live up to the trust that had been placed in them.

They worked tirelessly to strengthen the bonds of community, to provide support and resources to those who were struggling, and to ensure that no one in Slaughter would ever again have to suffer in silence and isolation. And though the road ahead was long and difficult, they knew that they would walk it together, united in their commitment to one another and to the enduring values of compassion, empathy, and love.

As the residents of Slaughter, Louisiana went about their daily lives, blissfully unaware of the dark secrets that lay hidden in their midst, a sickening stench began to permeate the air. It was a smell that defied description, a noxious blend of decay, waste, and something far more insidious - the unmistakable odor of death.

For years, Lacey Fletcher had been a familiar sight in the small town, a vibrant young woman who could often be seen power walking through the neighborhood, a pair of dumbbells clutched tightly in her hands as she worked to maintain her impressive physique. But as time passed and Lacy's presence on the streets grew increasingly rare, her neighbors began to wonder what had become of the once-active 30-year-old.

When Robert Slade, a longtime resident of Slaughter, casually inquired about Lacy's whereabouts during a chance encounter with her father, Clay Fletcher, he was met with a terse and evasive response. "Oh, uh, no, she's still here," Clay muttered, quickly changing the subject before Robert could press him further.

But even as Clay sought to deflect attention away from his daughter's mysterious absence, the truth of Lacy's horrific fate was slowly beginning to seep out into the world. Unbeknownst to her neighbors and friends, the young woman had become a prisoner in her own home, her body fused to the couch where she lay in a state of unspeakable neglect and degradation.

As Lacy's condition deteriorated and her body began to break down, the telltale stench of death began to waft through the Fletcher household. It was a scent that defied easy categorization, a complex and overpowering miasma of more than 800 different chemical compounds that reacted with the air and with each other to create a uniquely sickening aroma.

To those who have encountered the smell of death firsthand, it is an odor that can never be forgotten. Underneath the more immediate notes of fecal matter, waste, and decay - the kind of stench one might associate with a piece of raw meat left to rot in the sweltering heat of a cramped and poorly ventilated space - there lies a peculiar sweetness, an almost cloying undertone that seems to cling to the back of the throat and linger in the nostrils long after the initial shock of the stench has passed.

For the first responders and investigators who would eventually be called to the scene of Lacy's tragic demise, the overpowering odor of death would serve as a grim and unforgettable reminder of the unimaginable suffering that the young woman had endured in her final days. As they picked their way through the squalid and filthy living space where Lacey had spent her last moments, the sickening stench of secrets and lies mingled with the unmistakable reek of a body in the advanced stages of decomposition.

But even as the shocking details of Lacy's ordeal began to emerge, the people of Slaughter found themselves grappling with a sense of profound unease and disbelief. How could such an unspeakable tragedy have unfolded right under their noses, in a town where everyone knew everyone else's

business and where the bonds of
community were supposed to be
unbreakable?

The Fletchers

In the quaint, close-knit town of Slaughter, Louisiana, Sheila Fletcher stood out as a beacon of leadership and compassion. As one of the town's esteemed aldermen and the vice mayor, Sheila embodied the very essence of what it meant to be a pillar of the community. Her unwavering dedication to her neighbors and her tireless efforts to foster a sense of unity and support among the town's residents had earned her the respect and admiration of all who knew her.

Alongside Sheila, her husband Clay was equally renowned for his commitment to the community. As a prominent member of the Baton Rouge Civil War Roundtable, a nonprofit organization dedicated to preserving the region's Civil War heritage, Clay sought to promote a deeper understanding and appreciation of the town's rich historical legacy. Clay remained steadfastly focused on the organization's core mission of education and outreach.

Together, Sheila and Clay were the go-to couple for anyone in Slaughter who found themselves in need of assistance or support. Whether it was a neighbor grappling with a personal crisis or a family struggling to care for an ailing loved one, the Fletchers were always there to lend a helping hand and a sympathetic ear. Their boundless compassion and selfless devotion to the well-being of others had become the stuff of legend in the tight-knit community, a shining example of what it meant to truly care for one's fellow human beings.

But even as the Fletchers poured their hearts and souls into the service of their beloved town, a dark and troubling mystery was slowly unfolding within the walls of their own home. It had been years since anyone in Slaughter had laid eyes on the couple's young daughter, a vivacious and athletic girl who had once been a fixture of the town's streets and sidewalks. For Robert Slade Sr., a longtime neighbor of the Fletchers, the last memory he had of the girl was a fleeting glimpse of her jogging down the road, a pair of dumbbells clutched tightly in her arms as she pushed herself through a rigorous workout routine.

As the years stretched on and the girl's presence in the town grew ever more scarce, the people of Slaughter began to speculate about her whereabouts. Some whispered that she had gone off to college in the big city, trading the slow pace of small-town life for the bright lights and boundless opportunities of the urban world. Others mused that she had fallen in love and gotten married, starting a new life and a family of her own far from the place where she had grown up.

But for Robert Slade Sr. and a handful of other neighbors, there was a nagging sense that something wasn't quite right. It seemed almost inconceivable that a young woman who had once been such a vibrant and active presence in the community could simply vanish without a trace, leaving behind no clues or explanations for her sudden and prolonged absence.

The people of Slaughter found themselves grappling with a growing sense of unease and uncertainty. What could have happened to the Fletchers' daughter, and why had no one in the town seen or heard from her in so long? Were there dark secrets lurking beneath the surface of this seemingly idyllic community, hidden truths that threatened to shatter the carefully cultivated image of harmony and togetherness that the town had worked so hard to maintain?

Only time would tell what had become of the missing girl, and what role, if any, her disappearance might play in the larger tapestry of tragedy and despair that was slowly beginning to unravel the very fabric of Slaughter's close-knit world. But one thing was certain: for Sheila and Clay Fletcher, the weight of their own unspoken secrets and unresolved pain was growing heavier by the day, a burden that threatened to consume them even as they struggled to maintain their roles as pillars of the community and guardians of its most vulnerable members.

The Couch of Horrors

As Dr. Bickham approached the unassuming white house on that fateful day in January 2022, he could scarcely have imagined the horrors that awaited him within. The small town of Slaughter, Louisiana, was still bedecked in the cheerful trappings of the holiday season, with Christmas trees and New Year's decorations lending an air of festive normalcy to the humid, oppressive atmosphere. But as the doctor stepped out of his car and made his way up the well-manicured lawn, he had no way of knowing that he was about to stumble upon a scene of unimaginable squalor and neglect.

The moment Dr. Bickham opened the front door, he was hit with an invisible wall of stench that nearly knocked him off his feet. The overpowering odor of feces, urine, and the unmistakable reek of death permeated every corner of the house, clinging to the very fabric of the walls and furniture like a noxious miasma. Despite his years of experience in the medical field, the doctor found himself struggling to catch his breath, his lungs burning with the acrid tang of human waste and decay.

As he made his way into the living room, Dr. Bickham was struck by the strange and unsettling contrast that greeted him. Most of the room appeared to be relatively tidy. It was clear that someone in the household had taken great pains to maintain a semblance of normalcy and order, dutifully cleaning and arranging the various knick-knacks and decorations that adorned the shelves and tables.

But at the center of the room, like a festering wound that refused to heal, sat the dark brown leather couch that would soon become the stuff of nightmares. The couch was the source of the ungodly stench that had assaulted Dr. Bickham's nostrils from the moment he entered the house, and as he drew closer, he could almost see the steam rising from its surface, as though the very fabric of the furniture was slowly melting away before his eyes.

The couch was soaked through with urine and feces, the pungent waste oozing from every pore and crevice of the once-plush leather. The human excrement had seeped through the bottom of the couch and onto the floor below, where it had pooled in a fetid, stagnant puddle that seemed to pulse with a sickening life of its own. It was clear that no one had made any attempt to clean the area beneath the couch in a very long time, and the floorboards themselves appeared to be on the verge of crumbling away entirely, weakened by the constant exposure to the corrosive waste.

For Dr. Bickham, who had witnessed his fair share of gruesome scenes throughout his career, the sight of the couch was like nothing he had ever encountered before. It was a testament to the depths of human depravity and neglect, a symbol of the unimaginable suffering that had taken place within the confines of this seemingly ordinary suburban home.

Dr. Bickham couldn't help but wonder about the chain of events that had led to this moment. Who was responsible for allowing another human being to languish in such squalid conditions for so long? What could possibly drive a person to ignore the most basic needs of their own flesh and blood, to let them waste away in a prison of their own filth and misery?

These were questions that would haunt the doctor long after he had left the fetid confines of the Fletcher home, questions that would gnaw at his conscience and keep him awake long into the night. For now, though, his only thought was to do whatever he could to alleviate the suffering of the poor soul who lay trapped within the clutches of that accursed couch, to offer what little comfort and dignity he could in the face of such overwhelming despair.

Little did Dr. Bickham know that the true extent of the horrors lurking within the Fletcher household had only just begun to reveal themselves, and that the road ahead would be fraught with unimaginable trials and revelations. But in that moment, as he stood transfixed by the couch of horrors that seemed to pulse with a malevolent energy all its own, one thing was certain: the lives of everyone involved in this grim and twisted tale would never be the same again.

The Horrifying Discovery

As Dr. Bickham cautiously approached the source of the overpowering stench that permeated the Fletcher home, he found himself confronted with a scene that defied all reason and humanity. There, in the center of the living room, sat a couch that had become a grotesque parody of its intended purpose, a festering tomb that had swallowed up the broken and wasted body of Lacey Fletcher.

The couch itself was a nightmarish sight to behold, its once-plush leather now mottled and discolored, oozing with the accumulated filth of years of neglect and depravity. A large gap separated the couch from the wall, and in that narrow space, the very air seemed to shimmer with the noxious vapors that rose from the puddle of liquid waste that had gathered there. The wall itself was slick with moisture, as though the very house were weeping in horror at the atrocities that had been committed within its walls.

But it was the figure of Lacey Fletcher herself that truly stopped Dr. Bickham in his tracks. She was not so much lying on the couch as she was embedded within it, her emaciated form sunk deep into a person-sized crater that had been worn away by years of constant pressure and decay. Her body was twisted and contorted, her legs crossed in a grotesque parody of repose, her arms hanging limply at her sides.

Most horrifying of all were Lacy's eyes and mouth, both frozen wide open in a silent scream of agony and despair. Her face was a mask of suffering, her features almost unrecognizable beneath the layers of filth and grime that caked her skin. She was naked save for a small, blue-patterned top that had been haphazardly pulled over her chest, leaving her lower body exposed in all its wretched glory.

But even that small measure of modesty could not conceal the true extent of the horrors that Lacey had endured. Her body was a ravaged wasteland, her bones protruding at sickening angles through skin that had been eaten away by the very maggots that still crawled and writhed across her flesh. The sight of those tiny, wriggling creatures burrowing into the rotting meat of her body was enough to turn even the strongest of stomachs, and Dr. Bickham found himself fighting back a wave of nausea as he struggled to comprehend the sheer depravity of what lay before him.

As he drew closer, the true extent of Lacy's suffering became even more apparent. Feces and urine covered every inch of her body, caked into her hair and her ears, even filling her mouth and stomach. It was clear that she had been living in her own waste

48

for an unimaginable length of time, either too weak or too broken to even attempt to clean herself.

The sofa arms bore the telltale scratches of a person who had been desperately trying to claw their way free, a testament to the years of torment and isolation that Lacey had endured. And as Dr. Bickham looked closer, he realized with a sinking sense of horror that this was no ordinary case of neglect or abuse.

Lacey Fletcher had not simply been left to die on that couch, her body rotting away in the aftermath of her passing. No, the truth was far more sickening, far more unimaginable than that. For 12 long years, Lacey had been kept alive in this state, trapped in a prison of her own waste and despair, unable to even rise to use the bathroom or feed herself.

The realization was like a punch to the gut, a blow that left Dr. Bickham reeling with shock and disbelief. What kind of monster could subject another human being to such unimaginable cruelty, such utter debasement of the human spirit? What twisted and evil force could drive a person to inflict such horrors upon their own flesh and blood, to watch them waste away in agony and filth for more than a decade?

As he stood there, transfixed by the sight of Lacey Fletcher's ravaged and broken body, Dr. Bickham knew that he was standing at the threshold of a horror beyond anything he had ever encountered before. And in that moment, he vowed to do whatever it took to unravel the twisted and sickening mystery that had led to this moment, to bring those responsible to justice and to finally grant Lacey the peace and dignity in death that had been so cruelly denied to her in life.

The Façade of Care

even as the full extent of Lacy's suffering was laid bare for all to see, her parents,

Sheila and Clay Fletcher, seemed to remain strangely detached and unconcerned. As they stood in the kitchen of their home, mere feet away from the couch where their daughter had wasted away in agony for 12 long years, they offered no explanation for their actions, no hint of remorse or regret for the unimaginable torment they had inflicted upon their own flesh and blood.

It wasn't until weeks later, when Sheila Fletcher was finally questioned by police, that the true depths of the family's dysfunction and denial began to come into focus. In a shocking display of callousness and self-delusion, Sheila attempted to paint a picture of Lacey as a troubled young woman who had simply chosen to withdraw from the world, a recluse who had stubbornly refused all offers of help and support from her loving and dedicated parents.

According to Sheila, Lacey had struggled with social anxiety and mental health issues since she was a teenager, and had even sought treatment from a psychologist for a brief period of time. But despite their best efforts to get their daughter the help she needed, Sheila claimed, Lacey had ultimately chosen to retreat into a world of her own making, refusing to leave the couch or engage with the outside world in any meaningful way.

To hear Sheila tell it, she and Clay had done everything in their power to accommodate Lacy's wishes, going so far as to set up a makeshift toilet next to the couch and provide her with all the creature comforts she could possibly need. They brought her fresh changes of clothes, stacks of her favorite movies to watch, even baby wipes and powder to help her maintain some semblance of hygiene and dignity.

But as the interview wore on, the cracks in Sheila's carefully crafted façade began to show. She spoke of having to clean Lacy's body and bed sores on a regular basis, of changing out the towels that Lacey used as a makeshift toilet when they became too soiled with feces and waste. And yet, incredibly, she maintained that Lacey had never once complained of pain or discomfort, even as her body was quite literally rotting away beneath her.

It was a claim that strained credulity to the breaking point, a sickening and self-serving lie that laid bare the depths of Sheila and Clay's moral bankruptcy. For how could any parent, any human being with even a shred of decency or compassion, stand by and watch as their child wasted away in such unimaginable agony, their body eaten away by maggots and their spirit broken by years of isolation and neglect?

As the investigation into Lacy's death continues to unfold, it is becoming increasingly clear that the Fletchers' callous indifference to their daughter's suffering was not simply a case of ignorance or misguided love, but a fundamental failure of the most basic duties of parenthood. And while the full extent of their culpability in Lacy's tragic fate remains to be seen, one thing is certain: the façade of care and concern that they so carefully cultivated has been irreparably shattered, revealing the ugly truth of a family that had long since abandoned any pretense of humanity or compassion.

Dubious Claims

The credibility of Sheila Fletcher's account comes under increasing scrutiny. According to Sheila, Lacey had lost her appetite in the autumn of 2021, yet she claims to have provided her daughter with a meager meal of half a sandwich and a bag of Cheetos on January 2nd, 2022, just one day before her tragic demise.

However, the autopsy results paint a starkly different picture. Upon examination of Lacy's stomach contents, no trace of the alleged sandwich or Cheetos was found. Instead, the coroner discovered a grim mixture of sofa foam and feces, a disturbing indication of the depths of neglect and despair that characterized Lacy's final days.

The inconsistencies in Sheila's narrative raise troubling questions about the veracity of her claims and the extent of her involvement in her daughter's prolonged suffering. If, as the evidence suggests, Lacey had been confined to the couch for a staggering 12 years, the notion that she suddenly regained her appetite and consumed a meal prepared by her mother strains credulity to the breaking point.

Moreover, the notion that Sheila could have slept peacefully in a chair next to the rotting hole where her daughter lay trapped and dying is simply unfathomable.

The stench of decay and human waste would have been overpowering, a constant and inescapable reminder of the unimaginable suffering that was taking place just inches away.

As the true timeline of Lacy's ordeal begins to take shape, the sheer scale of her physical and psychological torment becomes ever more apparent. If, as the coroner suggests, her confinement began around 2010, the agony she endured in the intervening years is almost beyond comprehension.

Prolonged exposure to urine and feces is known to cause severe skin irritation and painful rashes, a condition commonly known as diaper rash in infants. Left untreated, these rashes can quickly escalate into full-body fevers, chills, and potentially life-threatening infections.

For Lacy, who was forced to sit cross-legged in a festering pool of her own waste for years on end, the risk of developing these agonizing conditions would have been incredibly high. The ammonia present in urine and feces is highly corrosive, capable of causing burns and open sores that would have left her in constant, excruciating pain.

As the years wore on and Lacy's body began to break down under the weight of her own filth and neglect, the physical and psychological toll would have been unimaginable. If, as some have suggested, she was still menstruating during the early stages of her confinement, the presence of blood in her waste would have attracted flies and other insects, adding yet another layer of torment to an already unbearable existence.

The image of Lacy, her body wracked with pain and her mind slowly unraveling, being forced to endure the constant buzzing and biting of flies drawn to the stench of her own rotting blood is one that will forever haunt those tasked with unraveling the mystery of her final days.

As the investigation continues and more details emerge about the true extent of Lacy's suffering, it becomes increasingly clear that the web of deceit woven by her alleged caregivers is beginning to unravel.

The Silent Killer

Lying amid the squalor and decay, young Lacey Fletcher endured agonies that extended far beyond the tortuous conditions surrounding her withered body. For in addition to being perpetually marinated in her own waste, the cruel reality of her unending confinement unleashed another insidious menace - one that invariably consumed the immobile from the outside in.

They were called decubitus ulcers, or more commonly, pressure sores. These malignant lesions emerged whenever constant, unrelenting pressure cut off blood flow to any part of the body for too long. Starved of oxygen and vital nutrients, the affected skin and underlying tissues began to die, giving rise to agonizing wounds that burrowed ever deeper if left untreated.

For Lacy, stranded unmoving upon that putrescent sofa, the appearance of such ulcers was an inevitability. Within just a couple hours of continuous pressure on her battered backside, the fragile skin would first redden and burn like a severe sunburn - an early warning of the trauma to come.

Left to fester, those inflamed patches would darken into murky purple blotches before finally rupturing, giving way to suppurating craters of decaying flesh that seeped foul, infected fluids. As the necrosis spread ever inward, even Lacy's muscles and bone became vulnerable to this advancing consumption, until entire chunks of her body had been transformed into cavernous, rotted pits offering a sobering vista into the exposed remnants of her inner anatomy.

The relentless pain and discomfort wrought by such pressure ulcers is considered among the most excruciating conditions an ailing body can endure. Yet for Lacy, the emergence of these virulent lesions across her motionless form only compounded the torment of her around-the-clock submersion in urine and feces. Together, it was an all-consuming array of suffering from which even the most steeled psyche could scarcely escape unscathed.

Moreover, the presence of such gaping wounds exponentially increased Lacy's susceptibility to contracting a deadly systemic infection. Sepsis, that insidious poisoning of the bloodstream, trailed these putrid ulcerations like a silent specter hungering for the kill that could finally end the wretched girl's unending misery and devastation.

The most unforgivable aspect of these horrors, however, was the chilling reality that they were completely preventable with only the most basic attentions. In proper care facilities, immobile residents are painstakingly rotated and repositioned every few hours to relieve sustained pressure and halt the onset of such lesions before they can take ruinous hold.

Yet for Lacy, utterly dependent upon her monstrous parental guardians, not even the most rudimentary preventative measures were taken to safeguard her delicate frame from this scourge of inertia. She was simply discarded, a human afterthought shunned to deteriorate amid the putrescence of her own bodily slimes and toxins.

As Lacy's motionless form was gradually devoured from all sides by this ruthlessly avoidable onslaught, it became hauntingly apparent that the failures enabling such nightmarish neglect extended far beyond the calculations of any one diseased parental psyche. For if our society's alleged humanitarian values could so utterly abandon a helpless young girl to endure the most abominable disintegration of her very physical essence, one is left to dread how many other untold victims have been forsakenly cast into similarly inhumane hells.

In this light, Lacy's remains stood not merely as an emblem of monstrous individualized sadism, but as a harrowing indictment against the repercussive indifference that enables such atrocities to persist in our very midst. Her sullied corpse cried out as the bodily revenant of all we have failed to changeours, until the whispers of her endless anguish find the resolve to at last displace our complacencies with a tenacity rivaling that which robbed her of peace.

The Macabre Symphony of Decay

Here is a prolix chapter with a true crime psychological tone about the events described in the transcript:

Chapter 17: A Waking Nightmare of Necrosis

The stench of decay permeated every crevice of that accursed dwelling, a miasma so thick one could practically taste the putrefaction on their tongue. As investigators breached the threshold, they bore witness to the full, grotesque extent of the horrors endured by the piteous Lacy. Her emaciated, supine form lay crusted with congealed bodily waste and alive with squirming masses of larvae.

What should have been the soft, supple flesh of youth was instead a grotesque landscape of suppurating sores and necrotized tissue. The proliferation of gangrenous lesions across her backside told a hideous tale of unimaginable neglect - of untold stretches spent wallowing in her own filth until the relentless onslaught of enzymes and bacteria had quite literally devoured away at the living matter.

So advanced was the necrosis that the boundaries between wounds and anatomy had dissolved into a seamless horror. What remained of Lacy's thighs and buttocks were mutilated beyond recognition, the flesh autobiography reduced to a jumbled palimpsest of oozing sores and dimpled craters pocked into the viscera. Even her mottled, jaundiced hide offered scant indication that this piteous creature had ever passed for human.

While the depravities inflicted upon the girl's body were manifold, one perverse cruelty stood as a harbinger of mercy amidst the brutalities. For by decimating the nerve endings across such a panorama of ravaged tissue, perhaps - mercifully - the capacity for anguish had been leached from these desecrated territories. Perhaps these zones of torture, scorched earth in the war against her own stricken vessel, had finally transcended into realms of pure insensation after a dozen torturous revolutions about the burning orbit of agony.

The only succor afforded the moribund innocent came in the form of an unholy alliance with those architects of bodily disintegration - maggots. Powered by insatiable hunger for the dead and dying, these singular scavengers had inadvertently stayed the rot through their relentless consumption of sloughing matter. Excavating each fistula, each ulcerous pit left by the onslaught of brute neglect, the verminous horde accomplished what Lacy's own progenitors could not - or would not.

With each mouthful of fetid flesh rendered into biomass and offal, the unassuming ranks of the fly larvae forestalled the inevitable triumph of sepsis. This blasphemous symbiosis, unspoken and unsolicited, had temporarily inoculated the sacrifice against the metabolic harrowing that surely loomed. For though every gobbet cast off from her blighted chassis taunted starvation's cold embrace, each nanosurge of new growth in the birthing pits of the flies gelled like a force-field against the splayed anatomy's absolute undoing.

The Whispers of a Wasted Life

Entombed within the putrid confines of that blighted dwelling, young Lacey Fletcher languished as little more than a vacant corporeal vessel amid the unrelenting onslaught of her own bodily degradation. Forsaken to the merciless reality of perpetual hunger and thirst, her frail existence steadily contracted into a singularity of primal desperation with each agonizing cycle. For with no nourishment within her circumscribed reach beyond the repulsive detritus enclosing her withered form, Lacy's starving body broadcast its lamentations through the sole available conduit - a grotesque grasping toward any potential source of caloric relief, no matter how depraved.

It was this grim reality that the forensic autopsy laid bare, as the dissection of Lacy's wasted anatomy disgorged the profane evidence of Life's cruelest declining act - tattered masses of synthetic sofa stuffing, the only vicarious matter her feeble extremities could grasp in a futile effort to placate starvation's tyrannical "voice." Where wholesome foods and hydrating liquids should have fortified her dwindling reserves, only this unnatural polymerized chaff found passage into the permanent purgatory to which she was confined.

Yet as unconscionably abhorrent as this compulsive ingestion was, it represented merely the outermost periphery of the expansive horrors conspiring to violently abbreviate Lacy's tenuous mortal grasp. For in the stark tallies that remained, her corporeal chassis had withered to a scarcely buoyant 96 lbs - a haunting cerulean diminuendo on the scales of vitality, offering visceral testament to the ruination wielded by malnutrition's unchallenged dominion.

And even as the death knells mounted with each degenerative nadir breached in Lacy's spiraling deterioration, the pathological cascades only intensified their malignant metastasis. Confined to the torturous continuum between nightmare and fitful terror-roused wakefulness, the helpless innocent's unremitting stasis allowed for the parasitic infestation of virulently invasive decubitus ulcers - malevolent lesions that steadily consumed ever deeper into the ravaged flesh with each compounding cycle of disregard.

So debilitating was this flesh-consuming pandemic that even the innermost sanctums of Lacy's skeletal ultrastructure fell prey to its septic disseminations, as purulent bone and marrow infections obliterated the last shielding resilience of her innate biological firewalls.

Ultimately, it was this unchecked conflagration of immunological civil war that presaged the definitive termination of Lacy's unthinkable entombment. Her tattered and failing corpus could no longer endure the overwhelming adversity of sepsis' exsanguinating recursions, however heinous her existence had become. And at some indiscernible horizon within the all-consuming malignancies burning away at her consciousness, the corrosive leaching of vitality snuffed out that feeble spark of sentience in a dull sputter of finality.

Yet echoing the eldritch paradoxes that haunted the anguished landscape of her life, disquieting uncertainties persisted regarding the full extent of Lacy's afflictions even after death's cessation. For by the obscured currents of fate's undisclosed diversions, the physical torments evidenced were perhaps destined to comprise only the briefest murmurs preceding a deeper, resonant chorus of revelation awaiting its whispered disclosures from the profouand apertures of perpetuity.

While no treatment could ever be administered to retroactively alleviate the profound sadisms Lacey Fletcher endured with each ephemeral respite, the exhumation and public reckoning of her full narrative stands as perhaps the sole inoculation against any insidious resurgence of society's most malignant pathologies. For in bearing seared witness to these far extremities of human indecency, we may paradoxically acquire the catalyzing impetus to demand systemic reformation - to unequivocally deracinate the fomentations that conspired in braiding this most abhorrent of tapestries.

Of course, certain tangential facets of Lacy's saga exhumed their own subsidiary undercurrents of bafflement - chief among them being the utterly inscrutable admissions of the alleged maternal element, Sheila Fletcher. With an air of cultivated nonchalance more befitting a farcical vaudevillian performer than reality's bleakest tragedies, the matriarch portrayed herself as a wholly detached observer to her very daughter's spiraling physiological and medical deterioration.

Proclaiming an apparently steadfast refusal to ever validate Lacy's cries for intervention with so much as a single professional assessment, Sheila's demeanor suggested either the hallmarks of acute sociopathic dissociation or a profound crevasse of ignorance more abysmal than any individually-aimed malice. Yet these rudimentary disavowals of her daughter's existential distress represent an auxiliary atrocity unto themselves - hallmarks of human frailty perhaps transcending the physiological husks they disregarded.

As investigators delved into appropriating these haunting revenants exhaled from the peripheries of Lacy's dissolution, it became jarringly evident that the parental imposition of her quarantined obscurity had persevered with an almost fanatical zealotry. For apart from a scantly populated handful of initial confidants, few in the immediate environs retained any inkling that the decrepit Fletcher premises played grim host to more than a soulless façade of derelict vacancy.

Only from the wistful remembrances of Lacy's childhood peers and outlying witnesses could the shards of her once-vibrant identity be exhumed from the disinterring repositories of posterity's recollections.

These oral histories depicted a specter far removed from the grotesque afterimage burned into present tense - that of an animated, amiable, and eminently sociable young entity brimming with sincere affability and an effusive kernel of eager curiosities. A dynamism that imbued her earliest incarnations with infectious zest, likely persisting in desperation until the all-consuming dimness of her cicumstances ultimately subsumed that light into abject obscurity.

There is an encompassing visceral displeasure in juxtaposing these luminous vignettes against their looming abominable counterpoint, as it forces reckoning with the most tragic of paradoxes. Yet in obliging ourselves to heed these suppressed aspirations of zestful potential from the blight of their calamitous extinguishing, we may inexplicably rekindle the compulsions to forestall such obliterations once and for all.

For just as we resign ourselves as bereaved witnesses to these deepest abysses of seared indignity, it is from their charring residuals that we must harvest the unmistakable charge to consecrate an new reality - one where the abandoned can no longer conflagrate into the smoldering aftermath of such catastrophic harmonic erasures. An inevitability where the tentative yet lustrous sparks that now flare in each newly inculcated lifescape are permitted to fully immolate into radiant, all-consuming ardor - to let their halcyon incandescences repel the ponderous gloom with sunward apogees that compel us ever onward toward our highest accretions of being.

The Entombed Light

Even as the final years of Lacy's life descended into a waking nightmare of grotesque deterioration, faint echoes of the vibrant spirit she once embodied still resonated in the memories of those who knew her.

For the young Lacey found rapturous escapism in the whimsical worlds of Disney. Whether getting swept away by an animated musical's transporting melodies or expressing feverish admiration for the iconic cast of characters, Disney's magical realms beckoned her into a universe of wonder far from the mundane existence she inhabited. These imaginary lands were a sanctuary where her childlike sense of enchantment could freely blossom amid kaleidoscopic spectacles.

So immersive were these reveries that reality itself became Lacy's canvas to adorn with extraordinary touches. She eagerly shared digital gateways into Disney's pixelated wonderlands with friends, juggling equal admiration for the transcendent vocals of Mariah Carey. An insatiable yearning for the fanciful and transcendent burned within Lacy, shared diversions offering fleeting refuge from the dark confines of her daily existence.

Perhaps it was this very capability to become rapturously absorbed in realms of fantasy that allowed her fragile psyche to erect some dimly lit bulwark against the creeping miasma enveloping her harsh reality, for as long as reverie's faint ember could be stoked.

Yet Lacy's vibrant essence extended well beyond the domains of make-believe. An avid seeker of tactile experience and unbridled expression, she avidly pursued athletic indulgences like the kinetic cadences of bowling or the uninhibited dynamism of volleyball's acrobatics. Each represented an embodied celebration of her yearning spirit, a cry for transcendent immersion in life's physical abundances.

It was this tenacious zeal for living that burned brightest in the recollections of those who knew Lacey before the long shadow of torment cast its pall. In an age when adolescent disruptions are expected, she defied conventions with a paradoxically sunny, affable disposition that disarmed all exposed to her aura of sweetness and grace.

And yet, the nostalgic refrains extolling Lacy's communal essence rang in stark dissonance with the discordant proclamations from those closest to her - twisted parodies portraying an acutely introverted, withdrawn specter. It reflected more than mere terminological apathy regarding her autism diagnosis, but an insidious disregard for acknowledging and validating the very experiential prism through which her effervescent identity took form.

Only Lacy's childhood comrades offered true testament to her indigenous spirit of dynamism and unrestrained curiosity. Their reminiscences alone elevated the harmonics of her bright resonance above the din of disavowals that so muddied her origins story - indelible bruise-memories bearing witness to an uncompromising vitality that thrived on constantly challenging novelty and dismantling staid routines to ingeniously catalyze personal passions.

Yet when juxtaposed against the grim, petrifying afterimage of her eternal corporeal tomb, this vibrantly animated existential essence proffers both the ultimate tragic dissonance and a horrific indictment of society's failure to conscientiously champion every such individual's inner luminosity before it is systematically, permanently extinguished beneath the phyacteries of malign neglect.

For if this forsaken spark's obliteration represents the most abhorrent of societal transgressions, the only conceivable future penance lies in cultivating an unwavering vigilance - an inviolable dedication to preserving the sacred mystic uniquity shining forth from each consonant experiential verse before the void can eclipse its beauty in consummate, endless silence.

In other words, eternal defiance against permitting the magnificence of a kaleidoscopic diversity in individual perception and Being to be subsumed by the indifferent nihilism of a world that's grown too jaded to bear the spiritual suffering of endlessly rekindling the sacred,embered incandescing no matter how benighted the crevasse from which it arises.

The Disintegration Of Self

Even as nostalgic reverberations conjured echoes of Lacy's vibrant, singular spirit from her earliest emanations, accounts from other figures surrounding her formative origins cast an increasingly dissonant pall over the impressions of her fundamental essence.

Dr. Bickham, the town physician who had served as the Fletcher family's primary care provider during Lacy's youth, rendered starkly starker clinical assessments than most rose-tinted refrains. While childhood companions depicted an affable, if unconventional adolescent simply harboring unique fascinations, Dr. Bickham's records characterized Lacey as an acutely solitary creature consumed by "severe autism and social anxiety."

This disharmonious interpretation of her developmental status raises profoundly disquieting implications. For if even medical professionals entrusted with safeguarding her wellbeing subscribed to reductionist pathologizations of her idiosyncrasies, it suggests her everyday identity may have been inadvertently distorted and medicalized.

Certainly, Lacey exhibited proclivities that could appear neurodivergent through a neurotypical lens - her raptures into realms of childlike fantasy, fixations on atypical stimuli. Yet consensus among those who truly knew her depicts not a hopelessly insular recluse, but a vivacious participant yearning for immersion in life's cerebral and somatic wonders.

Her interests may have appeared asynchronous, but this discrepancy stemmed from a stubborn refusal to discard her childlike sense of amazement - an ardent clinging to the adventurousness so often leeched away by adolescent socialization. Friends affirmed her lucidity, labeling her "smart as hell." While she grappled with socioemotional adaptations, these obstacles didn't ostracize her presence - she was "invited over to watch Disney movies" and partake in adolescent communion.

Lacey merely occupied a slightly outward orbit from conformities, her individuality inspiring affection, not alienation. As one intimate attested: "she just had her own interests, I wouldn't hardly call that strange."

Which begs the question of what factors impelled Lacy's abrupt institutional isolation at age 16 - a pivotal juncture when most initiate independence. Thrust into homeschooled purgatory, hallmarks of autonomy were unilaterally excised. Sports, friendships, innocuous rituals amputated with neither justification nor supplemental support networks to forestall dissociative sequelae.

From cycle to cycle, explanations contorted into muddled rationales and contradictions. Autism's transient labels devolved into palimpsests of "worsening severity," yet lacking precursory exposition. Only Dr. Bickham's deflated recountings bore faint cohesion, of the Fletchers materializing to cite banalities like "Lacey is becoming reclusive" to vindicate her accelerating self-quarantine.

Curiously noted were implications that documentary "photos or videos" could have evidenced her deteriorations - a subtle rebuke of the willful blindness and abnegations obscuring her plight, or Dr. Bickham's own surrender to rationalizing disturbing intimations.

What's starkly clear is that around the onset of Lacy's isolation, insights into her essence became subsumed by mitigations, evasions, perversities. An obfuscational zeal so totalizing that any acknowledgement of the vanished innocent's well-being was ultimately excised from conversational memory.

Until eventually, the sole affirmation of Lacy's persisting existence were Dr. Bickham's obligatory visitations to chronicle the furthering cartography of her deterioration - each new disclosure about her obliteration excavated from the wasteland where any accounting of her dissipated spirit lay interred.

By the juncture her cadaverous remnants were unearthed, the malleable integuments on her posterior had been eroded and devoured, bequeathing a bizarre and unrecognizable panorama of decomposition.

Where once there had been the lithe undulations of her femurs and glutei, there now prevailed a grotesque mosaic of putrefying integument and denuded ossein, a somber attestation to the unremitting agony she had suffered. So progressed was the condition of decay that it was virtually unfeasible to discern where one constituent of her anatomy concluded and another commenced, her epidermis and underlying configurations having been so exhaustively despoiled by the perfidious advancement of necrosis and the rapacious cravings of the larvae that had made her frame their abode.

In the scarce localities where her tegument endured somewhat unscathed, it had assumed a morbid, jaundiced tint, an unequivocal portent of the unchecked contagions that had undoubtedly surged through her debilitated and susceptible physique. The decubitus ulcers that had eroded her flesh had delved profound, burrowing through strata of subcutaneous tissue and sinew until they attained the very bones below, leaving her a cavernous husk of her erstwhile self.

The unabating barrage of her own bodily effluvia, the caustic fusion of excrement and urine that had accumulated beneath her for untold moons or solar cycles, had exacted a harrowing toll on her already compromised skin. The once-salubrious tissue had been ravaged by the inexorable propagation of gangrene, the unmistakable hallmark of cellular expiration and deterioration. Where once there had been the rubicund luminescence of vitality, there now subsisted only the charred, necrotic vestiges of what had once been a crucial and flourishing component of her corporeal form.

Perchance the sole diminutive clemency in this unraveling dread was the feasibility that the annihilation of her nerve extremities might have spared her from the full onslaught of the anguish that must have accompanied such a cataclysmic and protracted disintegration of the self. One can only aspire that as the pressure lesions and contagions burrowed ever deeper into her flesh, they might have severed the gossamer filaments that conveyed the signals of agony to her encephalon, bestowing upon her some modest measure of reprieve from the incessant tribulation of her subsistence.

But even if she was spared the direst of the somatic agony, the psychological exaction of such a profound and macabre deterioration of the corpus is almost too appalling to envisage. To be ensnared within a decaying carapace, impotent to stir or emit a plea for succor as one's very flesh is slowly devoured by the forces of putrefaction and the voracious appetites of the insects that feast upon the deceased - it is a destiny that defies depiction, a phantasmagoria rendered manifest in the most visceral and petrifying of ways.

And yet, amidst the revulsion and the despair, there is a peculiar and unsettling irony to be discerned in the verity that it was the maggots, those reviled and repugnant creatures, that may have ultimately played the most consequential role in prolonging Lacy's existence. For as they delved deep into her lesions, consuming the necrotic tissue and detritus that would have otherwise served as a breeding ground for even more perilous infections, they were unwittingly performing a crude but vital form of debridement, expurgating the moribund and perishing flesh that menaced to poison her from within.

In the chronicles of medical lore, the employment of maggots to cleanse and mend wounds is a convention that dates back centuries, a primitive but often efficacious means of staving off the direst ravages of infection and decay. And while the very notion of such creatures feasting upon one's own frame is enough to imbue even the sturdiest of stomachs with revulsion, there is a grim and terrible fascination to the conception that they might have been the sole ones standing between Lacey and an even more horrific and agonizing demise.

But even as we grapple with the macabre realities of Lacy's plight, it is impossible to disregard the glaring and unconscionable failure of those who were supposed to be her custodians and guardians. That her progenitors could have stood by and observed as their own offspring was slowly consumed by the forces of decay, her body becoming a literal breeding ground for the very creatures that feast upon the deceased - it is a betrayal so profound and so unforgivable that it almost defies comprehension.

In the end, the saga of Lacey Fletcher is a chronicle of unimaginable suffering and neglect, a life truncated by the cruelty and indifference of those who should have cherished her most. And while the maggots may have played their own unwitting role in the grim unfolding of her fate, it is the actions - and inactions - of her supposed sentinels that will forever stand as a damning indictment of the depths of human depravity and the unimaginable toll of untreated pain and despair.

No, it is not an acceptable answer

But instead of showing any actual proof of Lacey's issues, the Fletchers just strolled into Dr. Bickham's office with nothing - no photos, no videos documenting their daughter's supposed never-leave-the-couch situation. Their vague descriptions made it sound more like Lacey had developed a severe case of agoraphobia than her usual autism.

Agoraphobia is a nasty anxiety disorder where people are absolutely terrified of any environment they deem unsafe or impossible to escape from. At its worst, sufferers become completely homebound, unable to step outside because the mere thought of leaving their safe space triggers panic attacks.

Agoraphobia typically starts with general anxiety and gets incrementally worse over time if left untreated. What may begin as discomfort in public spaces could gradually escalate into never leaving the house, or even a single room that becomes the sufferer's solitary "safe" zone.

While the Fletchers provided zero evidence, their claims painted a bleak picture that Lacey may have become a prisoner in her own home, maybe even trapped within the confines of her deteriorating mind's creation if agoraphobia had truly taken hold.

Of course, jumping to conclude it was simply agoraphobia would be premature. Clearly, there were layers of parental unreliability and potential coverups obscuring whatever amalgamation of issues were really afflicting Lacey as she disengaged from school, friends, and normal life.

Some theories tried using her autism diagnosis as a catch-all excuse for her downward spiral. But advocates warn that's an oversimplified take that doesn't track - autistic people can absolutely live independently and maintain abilities like conversing, socializing, pursuing interests alone, and navigating environments autonomously without something significantly traumatic occurring.

By most accounts, Lacey retained many of those functional capabilities right up until her alienation and total seclusion. Her autism descriptor alone couldn't adequately explain the stark descent from her once-amiable existence into complete psychological devastation.

What increasingly seemed apparent, however, was that at some critical juncture, the narrative threads surrounding Lacy's lived experience became hazily obscured, then burned away entirely from her immediate communities until only the most jarringly incongruous remnants persisted in haunting the material record.

Somethingobscenely massive and too darkly inscrutable to directly confront had evidently encroached upon Lacy's essence and consumed her from the world. The precise nature of this obliterating presence remained ineffable, but its radius began systematically enveloping all witnesses to Lacy's origins once she crossed the threshold into her 16th year - a new cosmological certainty rendering all other existential distortions perversely benign in comparison.

Here's the chapter rewritten in a straightforward true crime narrative style geared towards a younger female audience:

Chapter 24: Untangling the Mysteries

As more bizarre details about Lacy's downward spiral into total isolation came to light, many were quick to point to her autism diagnosis as a simple explanation. "Oh, it must be because of her autism" was a common refrain. But experts and advocates pushed back hard on reducing her tragic unraveling solely to her neurodivergence.

"That's just not how autism works," they warned. There was little to no evidence justifying the extreme decision to pull a capable teenage girl entirely from school, friends, and critical support systems based on her diagnosis alone. The root causes prompting such a catastrophic alienation remained frighteningly unclear.

What could be pieced together painted a deeply disturbing timeline: At 16, Lacey disappeared from public life after her unexplained withdrawal from school. A handful of people like Robert Blad Sr. caught increasingly rare glimpses of her in passing until around age 21 when even those stray sightings ceased entirely.

It wasn't until Lacey turned 23 that her parents first admitted to Dr. Bickham she had become a complete recluse, refusing to leave the confines of their home. Yet just four years later at 27, reports indicated she still maintained enough functional capacity to digitally communicate with a friend.

This faint glimmer of autonomy didn't last. When inquiries about Lacy's well-being resurfaced around her 30th birthday, her parents gave a dismissive "she's fine at home" before shutting down further discussion.

Then, after six more agonizing years cut off from the world, the horrific discovery - Lacy's 36-year-old mummified remains were found decaying on that same couch, consumed by the very cushions that may have ultimately sealed her ghastly fate.

The apparent continuous nature of this terminal act - of Lacey sitting down on that couch one day and simply never getting up again until her body quite literally fused with the disintegrating fabric over more than a decade of unfathomable neglect - was perhaps the most viscerally haunting and incomprehensible aspect of the entire tragedy.

How could an able-bodied person with demonstrated physical capabilities simply decide to permanently plant themselves upon a piece of furniture until it literally devoured their flesh over the course of years? The very notion seemed to defy all logic and biological rationality.

Inevitably, outlandish theories began swirling online in an attempt to make sense of these glaring inconsistencies. One of the first to gain widespread traction was that Lacey may have suffered from "locked-in syndrome" - an extremely rare neurological disorder where the brain is fully conscious and aware but entirely paralyzed within an unresponsive physical prison.

If this had been Lacy's condition, the reasoning went, it could explain her gradual transformation into a barely animate fixture upon that couch, sentient yet utterly immobilized within the unforgiving confines of her own dysfunctional corporeal cage.

For a while, this medical diagnosis proved compelling enough for even major news outlets to embrace and report it as the definitive explanation for Lacy's decade-plus entombment. Framing her nightmarish ordeal as a known physiological phenomenon offered a tidy packaged rationale, discretely containing the more disturbing facets begging for reconciliation.

However, as more scrutinized details emerged, the locked-in syndrome theory rapidly disintegrated under the glaring holes it failed to address. Because even if Lacey had suffered such a catastrophic neurological event, certain documented capabilities seemed to definitively contradict its severe constraints.

Chief among them were her ability to facilitate digital communications, to orally ingest materials requiring at least minimal motor functions, and most damningly - her consumption of the very same sofa stuffing that eventually entombed her body. These complex physical actions indicated at least some intermittent operational capacities that simply could not exist within the totalizing paralysis of a textbook locked-in case.

So the convenient scenario reducing Lacy's plight to a grim yet comprehensible medical diagnosis began unraveling. Once again, it became clear the studied obfuscation surrounding her obliteration extended fractal-like into even more inscrutable depths - a basilisk event horizon whose true primordial catalyst continued eluding any singular, cohesive explanation.

The Inertia of Atrophy

Chapter 25: The Inertia of Atrophy

In the wake of the locked-in syndrome theory's unraveling, Dr. Bickham, the town physician who had intimate familiarity with Lacy's case, firmly refuted ever encountering such a diagnosis throughout his entire medical career. While an exceptionally rare neurological affliction, locked-in syndrome did not appear to align with the realities of Lacy's protracted disintegration.

This authoritative rebuttal only intensified the cacophony of bewilderment surrounding the most viscerally unsettling question of all: If Lacey did not suffer from total bodily paralysis, then what intervening forces or phenomena could possibly explain her inability to simply rise from that couch's accursed clutches across the 12 agonizing years she languished there?

Among the most prevalent conjectures was the grim possibility that, regardless of how Lacey initially became rooted upon the sofa, whether through coercion or incapacitation, the unremitting stasis and deprivations she endured initiated a self-perpetuating cyclone of physical atrophy from which escape became increasingly unattainable.

The human body, experts cautioned, reacts decisively to impeded mobility through a series of deteriorations if intervention is not administered. Even a temporary sedentary persistence can provoke uncomfortable parasthesias - the vexing "pins-and-needles" prickling that occurs when excessive localized pressure cuts off circulation to appendages. For able-bodied individuals, this uncomfortable tingling typically resolves once normal positions are resumed.

But if unabating confinement persists without the ability to alleviate compressive loads, the ramifications become exponentially more severe. Muscular atrophy, the progressive wasting away of nutrient-deprived and disused tissue, sets in at an alarming pace, potentially paralyzing the affected regions as they become locked into rigid atropic contractions.

In Lacy's hypothesized scenario of being confined to an immutable seated posture from the outset, the resulting onslaught of compounded peripheral traumas would have rapidly rendered any attempts at self-extrication physically impossible as her lower extremities withered into a rictus of fused, defunct lattices.

Exacerbating this catalytic myogelosis, the introduction of putrefying wounds and necrosis across the maximally loaded surfaces would only accelerate localized neuromuscular deficits. The suppurating cavities and lesions ravaging Lacy's lower posterior likely represented compoundingularly degenerative pathways through which any residual somatic facilitations were permanently compromised.

Indeed, the manner in which Lacy's body was ultimately discovered seemed to bear testament to these hypothesized mechanics of inertial degeneration.

Investigators noted her legs had become fusilladed into an acutely contorted cross-legged posture typically associated with defensive guarding against external antagonisms, rather than any innate positions of ambulatory facilitation or repose.

The profoundly disquieting implication was that even if Lacy's initial confinement had been self-imposed through some dissociative fugue or volition lapsus, the resulting tissue insults rapidly spiraled into a mutually reinforcing cyclone of abjectly compounding ruinations - each new breach skating ever farther outward toward the Eventually transgressed oblivion of her indissolubleAscesis.

Of course, any attempt at definitively reconstructing the primordial instantiation that inaugurated Lacy's carceral parallax remains an exercise in speculative conjecturalism, rife with probabilistic discoursions that rapidly degrade into hazier and ever dimmer luminousities of retrospective resolution.

For as inexorably as the physics of perpetual stasis seemed to have inscribed their cadaveric liturgies upon Lacey's being, the prospect of such an interminable petrification being enabled through solely internal dictates or agencies of volition appeared similarly implausible if not objectively denied to the furthest materialized vectors of salience.

Which served only to intensify the ultimate lapsing dissonances born of scrutinizing Lacey Fletcher's obliterative instance - the deepening chromatic snarls of measurable determinations encroaching into fractalizations of irreparably distorted discrepancy. Where each new hypothetical phototropism only unearthed collateral embrasures whose apertures to the obective eventualized as recursive dissimulations.

Leading invariably toward the conclusion that if any hope existed for rectifying the quandaries of how and through what infractored kinetics Lacey anamnesis became so cartographically subsumed, it would reside only in the profoundly ineffable dimensions. The first causes from which this degradationally vivific maleficence first germinated, and by whose most primordial resonances its reverberations may yet howl out from the abyssal continua.

The Insidious Perils of Prolonged Immobility

As the disturbing chronicle of Lacey Fletcher's ordeal continues to unfurl, one cannot help but ponder the myriad physiological perils that would have beset her body as a consequence of her protracted immobility. While online hypotheses abound, the grim reality is that within mere minutes or hours of assuming her fateful seated position, Lacey's circulatory system would have begun to falter, setting in motion a cascade of increasingly dire complications.

The sluggish flow of blood to her lower extremities would have swiftly given rise to the formation of pressure ulcers, those agonizing lesions that burrow deep into the flesh and underlying tissues. But this, alas, was merely the beginning of her torment. As the hours stretched into days and the days into weeks, the very tissues of her legs and buttocks would have begun to wither and die, starved of the vital oxygen and nutrients that sustain life.

In medical parlance, this phenomenon is known as a crushing injury, a term that belies the slow and insidious nature of the damage wrought upon the body. As the pressure on Lacey's limbs continued unabated, the cells and tissues within those compartments of her anatomy would have begun to break down, releasing toxins and waste products that would ordinarily be swept away by the flow of blood.

Chief among these byproducts was potassium, an electrolyte that plays a crucial role in the functioning of the heart and other vital organs. As the levels of potassium within Lacy's legs and buttocks continued to climb, her body would have been silently stockpiling a deadly payload, one that could be unleashed at any moment should the pressure on her limbs suddenly be released.

This is the cruel irony of the condition known as compartment syndrome, a potentially lethal complication of crushing injuries that occurs when the pressure within a confined space of the body rises to dangerous levels. Should Lacey have somehow found the strength to rise from her prison of flesh and bone, the sudden rush of potassium into her bloodstream could have triggered a catastrophic heart attack, snuffing out her life in an instant.

But even if she were to have survived this initial onslaught, the damage to her body would have been irreparable. By the time a year had passed, it is likely that Lacy's legs would have been rendered entirely useless, paralyzed by the inexorable march of tissue death and nerve damage. She would have been a prisoner within her own body, unable to flee the confines of the couch that had become her tomb.

And yet, the question remains: why did Lacey allow herself to sink into this abyss of immobility and despair? What could have driven her to remain in a position of such profound discomfort and peril, even as her body screamed out for relief? The answer, if indeed there is one, lies buried deep within the recesses of her psyche, a mystery that may never be fully unraveled.

Perhaps it was a manifestation of some underlying trauma or mental illness, a coping mechanism gone horribly awry. Or perhaps it was a reflection of the profound neglect and abandonment she had suffered at the hands of those who were meant to care for her, a final surrender to the hopelessness and despair that had consumed her soul.

Examining the Theories

The perplexing narrative of Lacey Fletcher's ordeal continues to captivate the public consciousness, and a multitude of hypotheses have emerged in an attempt to rationalize the unfathomable circumstances that led to her protracted and ultimately fatal confinement. Chief among these conjectures is the notion that Lacy's entrapment upon the couch was a product of her own volition, a manifestation of a debilitating mental affliction that rendered her incapable of extricating herself from the confines of her self-imposed prison.

According to this line of reasoning, Lacey may have fallen victim to a severe case of agoraphobia, a crippling anxiety disorder characterized by an irrational fear of open or public spaces. Proponents of this theory posit that the onset of Lacy's condition could be traced back to her teenage years, with the severity of her symptoms escalating exponentially with each passing year until the mere thought of venturing beyond the sanctum of her couch became an insurmountable obstacle.

Under this scenario, Lacy's parents, Sheila and Clay Fletcher, are cast in a marginally more sympathetic light, portrayed as well-meaning but hopelessly ill-equipped caregivers who found themselves increasingly overwhelmed by the intractable nature of their daughter's affliction. Some have suggested that the Fletchers may have initially dismissed Lacy's behavior as a manifestation of adolescent recalcitrance, a stubborn refusal to engage with the world beyond the confines of her chosen refuge.

As the years wore on and Lacey's condition continued to deteriorate, her parents' initial frustration and bewilderment may have given way to a sense of profound resentment and denial, a psychological defense mechanism that allowed them to distance themselves from the gravity of their daughter's plight. Proponents of this theory argue that the Fletchers' apparent neglect of Lacy's welfare was not born of malice or cruelty, but rather a product of their own emotional and psychological limitations in the face of an unimaginable crisis.

One piece of evidence that has been marshaled in support of this interpretation is the revelation that Lacy continued to communicate with her friends via email as late as 2014, when she would have been approximately 27 years old. According to reports, these missives bore all the hallmarks of Lacy's distinctive personality and passions, replete with effusive declarations of her love for all things Disney.

For those who subscribe to the theory of Lacy's voluntary confinement, these emails are seen as a tantalizing glimpse into the inner world of a young woman who, despite her profound isolation and deteriorating physical condition, remained capable of reaching out to those she held dear. They argue that the very existence of these communications casts doubt on the notion that Lacy was being actively abused or held captive against her will, as it seems improbable that her alleged tormentors would have allowed her to maintain such a connection to the outside world.

However, it must be noted that the provenance and authenticity of these emails remains a matter of considerable uncertainty. Without further information about the circumstances under which they were composed and transmitted, it is impossible to draw any definitive conclusions about Lacy's state of mind or the nature of her confinement during this period.

Moreover, even if one were to accept the premise that Lacy's retreat to the couch was a product of her own volition, the sheer scale and duration of her ordeal raises profound questions about the moral and legal culpability of those who were entrusted with her care. To suggest that the Fletchers were simply overwhelmed by the magnitude of their daughter's condition is to ignore the fundamental obligations of parenthood and to excuse a level of neglect that beggars belief.

Ultimately, the theory of Lacy's voluntary confinement, while perhaps superficially compelling, fails to account for the full complexity and horror of her situation. It is a narrative that seeks to impose a comforting logic upon a sequence of events that defies rational explanation, a desperate attempt to find some semblance of sense in a story that is, at its core, a testament to the depths of human suffering and the abject failure of those who were meant to protect and nurture a vulnerable young woman in her time of greatest need.

One of the most vexing aspects of this case is the apparent contradiction between the Fletchers' decision to seek medical advice regarding their daughter's increasing social withdrawal and their subsequent failure to intervene as her condition deteriorated to an unimaginable degree.

According to reports, Sheila and Clay Fletcher had, at some point prior to Lacy's death, approached Dr. Bickham to discuss their concerns about their daughter's growing tendency towards reclusiveness and isolation. This revelation raises a host of disturbing questions about the nature of the Fletchers' involvement in Lacy's plight and the extent to which they may have been aware of the severity of her condition.

If, as the evidence suggests, the Fletchers were sufficiently troubled by Lacy's behavior to seek professional guidance, why then did they not take more decisive action as the years wore on and her situation became increasingly dire? Why, instead of concocting a narrative of their daughter's supposed departure for college or marriage, did they not sound the alarm and seek more aggressive intervention on her behalf?

Some have posited that Lacy's autism may have played a role in her parents' apparent inability to recognize and respond to the severity of her condition. It has been suggested that individuals on the autism spectrum may struggle to articulate their pain and discomfort, leading to a potentially dangerous underestimation of their suffering by those around them.

However, this line of reasoning fails to account for the sheer horror of Lacy's physical deterioration, which would have been impossible to ignore even in the absence of verbal communication. The presence of gaping wounds, rotting flesh, and the grotesque spectacle of maggots feasting upon her body would have been an unmistakable sign of the utter depravity of her circumstances, regardless of any underlying neurological condition.

Others have speculated that Lacy may have developed a severe case of agoraphobia or even schizophrenia, which could have rendered her terrified of leaving the confines of her couch and highly vulnerable to the machinations of her own mind. Some have even gone so far as to suggest that a traumatic brain injury could have been the catalyst for her sudden and inexplicable behavioral shift, leaving her parents at a loss as to how to provide her with the care and support she so desperately needed.

But even if one were to accept these hypotheses as plausible explanations for Lacy's initial retreat into isolation, they do little to account for the Fletchers' abject

117

failure to intervene as her condition continued to worsen over the course of more than a decade. The fact that Lacy was able to survive for 12 years in such appalling circumstances suggests that she was receiving at least a modicum of sustenance and hydration, as well as some rudimentary form of dental care.

This paradox has led some to speculate that the Fletchers may have been so deeply in denial about the gravity of their daughter's situation that they were able to convince themselves that she was simply being stubborn or rebellious, rather than succumbing to a devastating physical and psychological breakdown. Perhaps, in their minds, they were acting as firm but fair parents, refusing to capitulate to what they perceived as their daughter's willful defiance.

But such a scenario strains credulity to the breaking point, as it requires us to accept that two individuals could have been so blinded by their own delusions as to ignore the utter devastation of their child's body and mind. It is a theory that paints the Fletchers as not merely negligent but actively complicit in the torture and degradation of their own flesh and blood.

some have sought to construct a narrative of parental concern and helplessness in the face of their daughter's inexplicable deterioration. They point to the presence of a toilet, baby wipes, clean clothes, and even Lacy's favorite movies as evidence that Sheila and Clay Fletcher were not merely neglectful monsters, but rather misguided caregivers struggling to come to terms with a situation that defied comprehension.

On the surface, these gestures of apparent kindness and consideration might seem to lend credence to the idea that the Fletchers were acting out of a sense of love and concern for their daughter, even as they failed to grasp the full horror of her condition. After all, why would they go to the trouble of providing her with these basic necessities and small comforts if they did not harbor some degree of affection and worry for her well-being?

But to accept this line of reasoning is to ignore the glaring inconsistencies and contradictions that lie at the heart of the Fletchers' behavior. It is to overlook the fact that, even as they were supposedly tending to Lacy's most rudimentary needs, they were also allowing her to waste away in a state of unimaginable squalor and degradation, her body riddled with gaping wounds and infested with the very creatures that feast upon the dead.

Moreover, the suggestion that the Fletchers may have been acting out of a sense of denial or ignorance about the severity of Lacy's condition is belied by their own actions and demeanor in the world outside their home. If, as some have suggested, they were simply unable to come to terms with the reality of their daughter's suffering, would they not have exhibited signs of this disconnect in their interactions with others?

Would they not have continued to speak of Lacy as if she were still a living, breathing presence in their lives, rather than a shameful secret to be hidden away from prying eyes? Would they not have sought out the comfort and support of friends and loved ones, even if only to unburden themselves of the terrible weight of their own guilt and confusion?

Instead, what we see in the Fletchers is a chilling pattern of secrecy and deception, a concerted effort to erase any trace of their daughter's existence from the public record. To their friends and acquaintances, Lacy had simply vanished, as if she had never been a part of their lives at all. There were no fond reminiscences of her childhood, no updates on her supposed college career or marital bliss - only a deafening silence that spoke volumes about the depths of their own apathy and neglect.

In the end, the theory of parental concern and denial in the Lacy Fletcher case is little more than a comforting fiction, a desperate attempt to impose some semblance of humanity and compassion upon a situation that defies all rational explanation. It is a narrative that seeks to absolve the Fletchers of their moral and legal culpability, to paint them as tragic figures caught in the grip of forces beyond their control.

But the reality of Lacy's ordeal is far more stark and unforgiving than any such mythology could ever hope to capture. It is a story of unfathomable cruelty and indifference, of a young woman left to rot in her own filth and misery while those who should have been her fiercest protectors looked on in silence.

No amount of baby wipes or clean clothes can erase the stain of that betrayal, nor can any gesture of apparent kindness mitigate the sheer, unmitigated horror of what Lacy was forced to endure. To suggest otherwise is to do a grave disservice to her memory, and to the countless other victims of abuse and neglect who suffer in silence, waiting for a world that all too often fails to hear their cries.

The online discourse surrounding the tragic case of Lacy Fletcher has given rise to a perplexing and deeply troubling narrative, one that seeks to cast her parents, Sheila and Clay Fletcher, in the role of helpless and overwhelmed caregivers, desperately struggling to cope with a situation that had spiraled far beyond their control. Some have even gone so far as to suggest that the Fletchers were themselves victims of circumstance, trapped in a nightmare scenario for which they were woefully ill-equipped and under-resourced.

But to accept this framing of events is to ignore the glaring discrepancies and inconsistencies that permeate every facet of the Fletchers' behavior. It is to overlook the fact that, far from being a family of modest means, the Fletchers had access to significant financial resources, as evidenced by their ability to post a staggering $72,000 in cash bail in the aftermath of their arrests. This alone would have been more than sufficient to secure Lacy a place in a long-term care facility, where she could have received the specialized attention and support that she so desperately needed.

Moreover, the notion that the Fletchers were isolated and alone in their struggle is belied by the close-knit nature of the Slaughter community, where neighbors and friends have a long-standing tradition of rallying around those in need. The idea that the Fletchers could have been suffering in silence for 12 long years, without a single person in their social circle taking notice or offering to help, strains credulity to the breaking point.

But perhaps the most damning indictment of the Fletchers' supposed helplessness lies in their own actions and demeanor outside the walls of their home. Far from being consumed by the demands of their caregiving responsibilities, Sheila and Clay Fletcher maintained an active and vibrant social life, cultivating a public image of warmth, generosity, and community engagement that stood in stark contrast to the unimaginable horrors unfolding behind closed doors.

This carefully crafted facade of normalcy and respectability is simply incompatible with the idea of the Fletchers as overwhelmed and under-supported caregivers. It is a testament to their capacity for deception and compartmentalization, their ability to present one face to the world while simultaneously perpetrating acts of unspeakable cruelty and neglect upon their own flesh and blood.

The fact that the Fletchers were able to maintain this illusion for so many years, to walk past their daughter's wasting body every single day without being moved to take action, is a damning indictment of their moral character and a profound betrayal of the most basic duties of parenthood. It is a level of callousness and indifference that defies comprehension, a testament to the depths of human depravity and the limitless capacity for self-delusion.

But the reality is far more stark and unforgiving. The Fletchers had every opportunity, every resource, and every incentive to intervene on their daughter's behalf, to seek out the help and support that could have saved her life. That they chose instead to stand by and watch as she slowly wasted away, her body ravaged by neglect and despair, is a testament to the depths of their own moral bankruptcy and the utter failure of their duties as parents and as human beings.

To suggest that Lacy's fate could have been avoided if only her parents had been given more support is to fundamentally misunderstand the nature of the evil that was perpetrated against her. It is to ignore the fact that, in the end, it was not a lack of resources or assistance that sealed her fate, but rather the cruelty, the indifference, and the utter lack of humanity of the two people who should have been her fiercest protectors and advocates.

No amount of community support or financial aid could have compensated for the moral and ethical void at the heart of the Fletcher household, nor could it have saved Lacy from the unimaginable torment she was forced to endure. Hers is a story of betrayal and abandonment, a searing indictment of the human capacity for evil and the devastating consequences of unchecked abuse and neglect.

Sinister Theory

The investigation into the tragic demise of Lacy Fletcher has given rise to a dark and disturbing narrative that has gained significant traction among law enforcement and the wider public. This theory posits that the young woman's prolonged ordeal was not the result of parental neglect or helplessness, but rather a calculated and deliberate campaign of torture and abuse at the hands of her own mother and father.

Central to this line of reasoning is the damning revelation that Sheila Fletcher, Lacy's mother, had outright lied to the police about the nature of her daughter's final meal. While Sheila claimed that Lacy had consumed a sandwich and a bag of Cheetos in the hours before her death, the autopsy results told a far more grim and unsettling story, casting serious doubt on the veracity of the Fletchers' entire account of their daughter's decline.

For many, this blatant act of deception was the final nail in the coffin of the Fletchers' credibility, exposing the depths of their callousness and depravity. What kind of parent would willfully mislead the authorities about the circumstances surrounding their own child's death, if not one with something truly sinister to hide?

Even as the theory of deliberate torture has gained traction, the exact nature and timeline of the alleged abuse remains shrouded in mystery and conjecture. Some have speculated that Lacy may have suffered a traumatic brain injury at some point in the past, perhaps at the hands of her own parents, leaving her unable to fend for herself or seek help from the outside world.

Others have suggested that Lacy may have been the victim of sexual abuse, and that her subsequent withdrawal and self-neglect were manifestations of the profound psychological trauma she had endured. These individuals point to the sudden and drastic shift in Lacy's behavior around 2010, when her parents reportedly sought the advice of Dr. Bickham regarding their daughter's increasing reclusiveness and isolation.

While these theories are purely speculative and based on limited evidence, they nonetheless paint a chilling picture of a young woman trapped in a nightmare scenario, at the mercy of the very people who were meant to protect and nurture her. The idea that Lacy's parents could have been responsible for inflicting such unimaginable suffering upon their own flesh and blood defies comprehension, showcasing the depths of human cruelty and depravity.

It must be acknowledged that the theory of deliberate torture is, at this stage, just that - a theory, unsupported by any concrete evidence or eyewitness testimony. However, the mere fact that such a scenario could be considered plausible by so many speaks volumes about the sheer horror and revulsion that this case has unleashed in the hearts and minds of the public.

For those who subscribe to this line of thinking, the Fletchers' behavior in the aftermath of their daughter's death is seen as a damning indictment of their guilt and complicity. The fact that they could have left Lacy to waste away in her own filth and misery for 12 long years, only to lie to the authorities about the circumstances of her final hours, is seen as evidence of a level of callousness and depravity that defies belief.

Even as the specter of torture and abuse looms large over this case, there is a sense among many that the full truth of what happened to Lacy Fletcher may never be known. The Fletchers have remained steadfastly silent in the face of the accusations against them, leaving a gaping void of uncertainty and speculation that may never be fully filled.

One thing is certain: the story of Lacy Fletcher is a searing indictment of the human capacity for cruelty and indifference, a haunting reminder of the unimaginable suffering that can be inflicted upon the most vulnerable among us. It is a clarion call for justice and accountability, a demand that the truth be brought to light, no matter how dark and disturbing it may be.

The investigation into this heinous crime continues to unfold, forcing us to grapple with the uncomfortable reality that the darkest and most depraved impulses of the human heart may lie behind the closed doors of even the most seemingly ordinary and respectable of homes. We must confront the fact that, for Lacy Fletcher and countless others like her, the greatest threat to their safety and well-being may come not from strangers or outsiders, but from the very people who are meant to love and protect them most.

This sobering and unsettling realization should give us all pause as we reflect on the fragility of the social fabric that binds us together. It is a reminder of the urgent need for vigilance and compassion in the face of evil, and for a steadfast commitment to justice and accountability, no matter how daunting the road ahead may be.

At the center of this tangled web lies the perplexing question of why Sheila Fletcher, Lacy's mother, would have called 911 to report her daughter's death, if indeed she and her husband were responsible for the young woman's horrific demise.

On the surface, this action would seem to be entirely inconsistent with the idea of a deliberate campaign of torture and abuse, a sadistic regime of cruelty and neglect that had been carefully hidden from the outside world for over a decade. After all, if the Fletchers had something so monstrous to conceal, why would they willingly invite the scrutiny of law enforcement and the glare of the public spotlight?

Some have suggested that the answer may lie in a chilling allegation made by one of the Fletchers' neighbors, a claim that has yet to be substantiated but that has nonetheless captured the dark imaginings of many who have followed this case. According to this theory, Sheila Fletcher may have been forced to make that fateful 911 call, not out of any sense of remorse or concern for her daughter's well-being, but rather under duress from an outside party who had stumbled upon the horrific scene inside the family's home.

The specifics of this alleged encounter remain hazy and unconfirmed, with some suggesting that the neighbor may have caught a glimpse of Lacy's wasted and decaying form through a window, while others speculate that they may have come knocking on the Fletchers' door, only to be met with a wall of silence and secrecy. Whatever the case may be, the idea that Sheila Fletcher's hand may have been forced by the threat of external intervention has added yet another layer of intrigue and uncertainty to an already deeply perplexing case.

But even if this theory were to be proven true, it would do little to explain the other inconsistencies and anomalies that have emerged in the wake of Lacy's death. The presence of toiletries, clean clothes, and other personal items in close proximity to the couch where she was found has been interpreted by some as evidence of a twisted form of psychological torture, a cruel juxtaposition of the basic human dignities that were being denied to her even as she lay slowly dying in her own filth and squalor.

Others have pointed to the disturbing detail of Lacy's partial nudity at the time of her discovery, with her shirt pulled up above her chest in a manner that many have seen as a final, sickening humiliation. The question of whether this was a deliberate attempt to degrade and dehumanize her in her final moments, or perhaps even a sign of something more sinister and unspeakable, has been the subject of much speculation and conjecture.

But perhaps the most troubling and perplexing aspect of this case lies in the fact that, despite the overwhelming evidence of neglect and abuse that was discovered at the scene, the Fletchers have yet to face any formal charges or legal consequences for their actions. The glacial pace of the investigation, and the apparent reluctance of local authorities to treat Sheila and Clay Fletcher as suspects in their own daughter's death, has only fueled the sense of outrage and frustration that has surrounded this case from the very beginning.

In the end, the truth of what happened to Lacy Fletcher may never be fully known, lost forever in the murky depths of human cruelty and depravity. But one thing is certain: the sheer scale and complexity of this case, with its tangled web of speculation, allegation, and inconsistency, is a testament to the enduring power of evil to confound and horrify us, even in an age when we like to believe that we have seen and understood it all.

As the investigation into this heinous crime continues to unfold, we are left to grapple with the uncomfortable truth that the darkest and most depraved impulses of the human heart may lurk behind even the most seemingly ordinary and innocuous of facades. We are forced to confront the fact that, for Lacy Fletcher and countless others like her, the greatest threat to their safety and well-being may come not from strangers or monsters, but from the very people who should have been their fiercest protectors and advocates.

The Surreal Spectacle Of Justice

As the legal proceedings surrounding the tragic case of Lacy Fletcher began to unfold, the sheer horror and disbelief that had gripped the community since the discovery of her body reached a new and utterly surreal level of intensity. The decision to bring the case before a grand jury, a group of ordinary citizens tasked with determining whether there was enough evidence to bring criminal charges against Sheila and Clay Fletcher, had been a long and arduous one, fraught with uncertainty and trepidation.

But as the jurors filed into the courtroom, their faces etched with a mixture of apprehension and grim determination, it quickly became clear that nothing could have prepared them for the sheer depravity and horror of the evidence that was about to be presented. Dr. Bickham, the coroner who had been one of the first to arrive on the scene of Lacy's death, had fought tirelessly to ensure that a team of medical professionals was on standby just outside the courtroom, knowing all too well the devastating impact that the images and testimony to come could have on even the most seasoned of observers.

As the district attorney began to lay out the timeline of Lacy's final years, the expressions on the faces of the jurors became a tableau of shock, revulsion, and utter disbelief. Some gasped audibly as the grotesque and heart-wrenching details of the young woman's ordeal were laid bare, their minds reeling at the thought of the unimaginable suffering she had been forced to endure. Others simply stared ahead in stunned silence, their eyes wide and unblinking, as if they could scarcely believe the nightmare unfolding before them was real.

For many in the courtroom that day, the idea that the Fletchers could have lived with the stench and squalor of their daughter's decay for so long was almost beyond comprehension. How, they wondered, could anyone have endured such an overpowering and sickening odor, day after day, without being driven to the brink of madness themselves? Some speculated that the couple might have developed a form of olfactory fatigue, their noses becoming so accustomed to the stench that they could no longer detect its presence. But even this explanation seemed to strain credulity, given the sheer magnitude of the neglect and degradation that Lacy had been subjected to.

As the proceedings wore on, the question of the Fletchers' ultimate fate loomed large over the courtroom. The grand jury, tasked with determining the appropriate criminal charges to bring against the couple, were faced with a daunting and unenviable choice. Should the Fletchers be charged with negligent homicide, a crime that would suggest that their actions, while reprehensible, were not intentional or malicious? Or should they face the far more serious charge of second-degree murder, an accusation that would paint them as cold-blooded killers who had knowingly and willfully subjected their own daughter to a torturous and agonizing death?

In the end, the decision would hinge on the question of intent, on whether the Fletchers had truly understood the depth and severity of their own cruelty, or whether they had been so lost in their own delusions and denial that they had convinced themselves that their daughter's suffering was somehow justifiable or unavoidable. It was a question that would likely haunt the jurors long after they had delivered their verdict, a moral and philosophical conundrum with no easy answers or tidy resolutions.

But for those who had borne witness to the unfathomable horror of Lacy Fletcher's final days, there was a growing sense that justice, in whatever form it might take, could never truly be enough. For the young woman who had suffered so greatly, and for the countless others like her who continued to languish in the shadows of neglect and abuse, the road to healing and redemption would be a long and difficult one, fraught with pain, anger, and an abiding sense of loss.

And yet, even in the face of such unimaginable darkness, there was a flicker of hope to be found in the fact that Lacy's story was finally being told, that the veil of secrecy and silence that had shrouded her suffering for so long was at last being lifted. It was a small and fragile thing, that hope, but it burned with the fierce and unquenchable light of truth, a beacon of justice and compassion in a world that all too often seemed to have forgotten the meaning of either.

As the grand jury prepared to render its decision, the eyes of an entire community, and indeed an entire nation, were fixed upon the proceedings, waiting with bated breath to see whether the arc of the moral universe would indeed bend towards justice. And though the road ahead would be long and fraught with uncertainty, there was a sense among all those present that day that they were bearing witness to something truly momentous, a reckoning that had been far too long in coming, but that could not be denied or delayed any longer.

Chapter Title: The Scales of Justice: Weighing the Charges and Consequences in the Lacy Fletcher Case

As the grand jury deliberated over the appropriate charges to bring against Sheila and Clay Fletcher, the legal and moral complexities of the case began to come into sharp and painful focus. At the heart of the matter lay the question of intent, the elusive and often inscrutable concept that would ultimately determine the severity of the accusations leveled against the couple, and the potential consequences they would face if found guilty.

On one end of the spectrum was the charge of negligent homicide, a crime that would suggest that the Fletchers' actions, while reprehensible and reckless, were not undertaken with the express purpose of causing Lacy's death. Under this interpretation of events, the couple's failure to provide their daughter with even the most basic level of care and human dignity would be seen as a tragic and inexcusable lapse in judgment, but one that stopped short of outright malice or premeditation.

If convicted of negligent homicide, the Fletchers could face a sentence of anywhere from zero to five years in prison, a punishment that many would likely view as woefully inadequate given the sheer scale and duration of Lacy's suffering. And yet, there were some who argued that even this outcome would represent a measure of justice for the young woman whose life had been so cruelly cut short, a recognition of the fact that her parents had failed her in the most fundamental and unforgivable of ways.

One step up on the ladder of culpability was the charge of manslaughter, a crime that would imply a greater degree of recklessness and disregard for human life on the part of the Fletchers. Under this interpretation, the couple's actions would be seen not as a mere lapse in judgment, but as a willful and unconscionable neglect of their most basic duties as parents and caregivers.

The classic example of manslaughter is often cited as a crime of passion, a situation in which an individual is driven to violence by a sudden and overwhelming surge of emotion, such as the discovery of a cheating spouse. In such cases, the perpetrator's actions are not premeditated or carefully planned out, but rather the result of a momentary loss of control and reason.

In the case of the Fletchers, the charge of manslaughter would suggest that their neglect of Lacy, while not necessarily undertaken with the express intent of causing her death, was so egregious and prolonged that it amounted to a reckless disregard for her life and well-being. If convicted of this crime, the couple could face a sentence of anywhere from zero to forty years in prison, a punishment that would reflect the severity of their actions and the irreparable harm they had inflicted upon their own child.

But for many who had followed the case and borne witness to the unimaginable horror of Lacy's final days, even the charge of manslaughter seemed inadequate to capture the full depths of the Fletchers' cruelty and depravity. In their eyes, the couple's actions amounted to nothing less than second-degree murder, a crime that would imply a level of intent and malice that went far beyond mere recklessness or negligence.

To illustrate the distinction between manslaughter and second-degree murder, the district attorney drew upon a chilling hypothetical scenario. Imagine, he told the jury, that an individual breaks into a home with the intent of burglarizing it, only to be confronted by the homeowner who unexpectedly returns. In a moment of panic and desperation, the burglar lashes out and kills the homeowner, a tragic and senseless act of violence that was never part of the original plan.

In such a case, the burglar could not reasonably claim that their actions were the result of a sudden and overwhelming provocation, as might be the case in a crime of passion. Rather, they had made a conscious and deliberate decision to engage in a dangerous and illegal act, one that carried with it the inherent risk of violence and death.

By the same token, the district attorney argued, the Fletchers' treatment of their daughter could not be dismissed as a mere lapse in judgment or a momentary failure of reason. Rather, it was the result of a sustained and deliberate pattern of abuse and neglect, one that had been carried out over the course of twelve long and agonizing years.

To allow Lacy to waste away in her own filth and misery, to watch as her body was slowly consumed by the forces of decay and the ravages of her own suffering, was an act of such unimaginable cruelty and malice that it could only be described as murder, plain and simple. And if convicted of this most serious of charges, the

Fletchers would face the prospect of life behind bars, a fitting and just punishment for the unimaginable torment they had inflicted upon their own flesh and blood.

As the grand jury weighed the evidence before them and struggled to reach a decision, the eyes of an entire community, and indeed an entire nation, were fixed upon the proceedings, waiting with bated breath to see whether justice would be served. And though the road ahead would be long and fraught with uncertainty, there was a sense among all those present that day that they were bearing witness to a reckoning that had been far too long in coming, a chance to hold accountable those who had so grievously failed in their most sacred and fundamental duties as parents and as human beings.

In the end, the charge of second-degree murder would carry the day, a recognition of the fact that the Fletchers' actions, while perhaps not premeditated in the strictest sense of the word, were nonetheless the result of a callous and deliberate disregard for their daughter's life and well-being. It was a verdict that would send shockwaves through the community and beyond, a powerful and unequivocal statement that such cruelty and neglect would not be tolerated, and that those who inflicted such suffering upon the most vulnerable among us would be held to account.

The Mockery of Mourning

Chapter Title: The Mockery of Mourning: Unraveling the Absurdity of the Fletchers' Plea for Privacy

As the legal proceedings against Sheila and Clay Fletcher began to unfold, the sheer audacity and absurdity of their public statements and actions became a source of mounting outrage and disbelief among those who had followed the tragic case of their daughter's death. Perhaps nowhere was this more apparent than in the comments made by the couple's attorney, Steven Moore, in the wake of their indictment on charges of second-degree murder.

In a statement released to the media, Moore attempted to paint the Fletchers as grieving parents, devastated by the loss of their child and desperate to avoid the glare of public scrutiny as they struggled to come to terms with their own unimaginable heartache. "They don't want to relive the pain of losing a child through the media," he declared, a sentiment that might have elicited sympathy or compassion under different circumstances.

But given the horrific nature of Lacy's suffering and the overwhelming evidence of the Fletchers' callous neglect and abuse, such a plea for privacy and understanding rang hollow and offensive to many. How dare these individuals, who had subjected their own daughter to such unimaginable torment and degradation, now seek to cloak themselves in the mantle of parental grief and sorrow?

To those who had borne witness to the grim details of Lacy's ordeal, the idea that the Fletchers could lay claim to the sacred and unimpeachable bond between parent and child was nothing short of obscene. What kind of parents, after all, could stand by and watch as their own flesh and blood wasted away in agony and squalor, her body consumed by the ravages of neglect and decay?

And yet, even as the Fletchers sought to portray themselves as victims of a cruel and unfeeling media, the reality of their own actions and choices painted a far different picture. The revelation that the couple had managed to scrape together a staggering $72,000 in cash to secure their release on bail, even as their daughter had been left to languish without medical care or basic human dignity for over two decades, was a damning indictment of their priorities and their capacity for self-preservation.

For many, this fact alone was proof positive that the Fletchers' neglect of their daughter was not the result of poverty, ignorance, or helplessness, but rather a conscious and deliberate choice to prioritize their own needs and desires over the most fundamental duties of parenthood. That they could have marshaled such resources to defend themselves against the consequences of their actions, even as they had failed to lift a finger to alleviate their own child's suffering, was a betrayal so profound and so unforgivable that it defied comprehension.

As the case against the Fletchers inches forward and the prospect of a trial looms on the horizon, the eyes of a nation remain fixed upon the proceedings, watching with a mixture of horror, anger, and grim fascination to see whether justice will be served. But even as the wheels of the legal system grind inexorably onward, there is a sense among many that the true scope of the Fletchers' crimes may never be fully reckoned or atoned for.

For the heartache and pain that they claim to have suffered in the wake of their daughter's death pales in comparison to the unimaginable torment that Lacy herself was forced to endure, alone and abandoned in the depths of her own private hell. That they could now seek to cloak themselves in the language of parental love and devotion, even as the evidence of their own monstrous neglect and cruelty mounts with each passing day, is a testament to the depths of human capacity for self-delusion and denial.

In the end, the case of Lacy Fletcher is a tragedy beyond measure, a story of unfathomable suffering and loss that will forever haunt the annals of true crime and the darkest recesses of the human heart. But it is also a powerful and urgent reminder of the sacred duties and responsibilities that we all bear towards the most vulnerable among us, and the terrible price that is paid when those duties are shirked or abandoned.

As the pursuit of justice for Lacy continues to unfold, let us all take a moment to reflect on the fragility of the bonds that bind us together as a society, and the vital importance of compassion, empathy, and shared humanity in the face of even the darkest and most unspeakable of crimes. For in the end, it is only by standing together in the face of such evil, and by reaffirming our commitment to the basic values of decency, dignity, and respect for all human life, that we can hope to build a world in which no one is ever again forced to suffer as Lacy Fletcher suffered, and in which the mockery of mourning is exposed for the hollow and self-serving sham that it truly is.

The very essence of parenthood is rooted in the sacred duty to protect, nurture, and care for one's offspring, to place their needs and well-being above all else, even in the face of the most daunting challenges or obstacles.

The idea that Sheila and Clay Fletcher could have stood by and watched as their own daughter wasted away in agony and squalor, her body ravaged by neglect and decay, is a betrayal of this most fundamental obligation that defies comprehension. That they could have been so consumed by their own pride, stubbornness, or selfish desires as to allow Lacy to languish in such unspeakable conditions for over a decade is a testament to the depths of human capacity for cruelty and indifference.

Even if one were to accept the Fletchers' dubious claim that Lacy had chosen this fate for herself, that she was in some way responsible for her own tragic decline, it would do nothing to absolve them of their moral and legal responsibilities as her caregivers and guardians. If anything, the notion that their daughter was suffering from a profound mental illness or disability that rendered her unable to make rational decisions for herself only heightens the degree of their culpability and neglect.

To dismiss Lacy's suffering as the result of her own stubbornness or willfulness, to insist that she was somehow complicit in her own degradation and torment, is an act of such breathtaking callousness and denial that it beggars belief. It is a narrativethat seeks to shift blame away from those who had the power and the responsibility to intervene, and onto the victim herself, a cruel and cowardly abdication of the most basic duties of parenthood.

In the end, there can be no justification or excuse for the Fletchers' actions, no mitigating circumstances or explanations that can even begin to account for the sheer scale and duration of their daughter's suffering. Whether born of sadism, neglect, or some toxic combination of the two, the reality of what Lacy endured at the hands of those who were meant to love and protect her is a horror that will forever stain the annals of human history, a searing indictment of the depths of depravity to which even the most seemingly ordinary individuals can sink.

The End

A quick re-cap, before we conclude this tragic story. Yes, there is a conclusion; but the extent of the suffering, the decay, and snuff is way too deep for us to simply forget it:

The stench inside that house was like nothing Dr. Vincent Bekom had ever experienced before. As the coroner, he'd seen his fair share of death over the years, but the overwhelming reek of sewage and rot told him this was something truly evil.

As he entered the living room, he was hit with a sight that will forever be seared into his memory. There on the couch was the withered, twisted body of a young woman. She had literally rotted away into a mummified corpse, contorted into an unnaturally posed position, like she had been stuck trying to escape from that depraved pit of filth.

Her vacant eyes told the story of prolonged suffering and anguish that no human being should ever have to endure. This wasn't just death - it was calculated, sadistic torture on an incomprehensible scale.

The revolting scene made it clear that Lacey hadn't simply succumbed to injuries or illness. She had been purposely forced to waste away for an agonizing length of time, slowly being devoured alive as she lay dying alone amid the squalor. The only semblance of sustenance was a tiny bag of hard candy - a cruel tease of relief that never came.

Over the next week, the images and putrid memories were seared into Dr. Bekom's mind, haunting his waking hours and denying him restful sleep. He had seen messed up things in his line of work, but nothing struck him as deeply human and soul-crushing as what was done to Laci.

Eventually, the full depravity came to light when Laci's parents - Clay and Sheila

Fletcher - were arrested and charged with her murder through calculated endangerment, torture, and starvation over a period of months or even years. In the final verdict, they were both found guilty of homicide and sentenced to decades behind bars.

But no prison sentence could make up for subjecting a young woman to that level of prolonged sadistic cruelty and evil. The nightmare of what Lacey endured in her final days will forever loom as an abject illustration of the profound darkness that can consume the human soul.

Made in the USA
Monee, IL
12 May 2024

58386102R00095